Give thanks to God who made us,
Who gave the birds their song;
Who made the world, and keeps it turning
All year long.

This book belongs to

_____

_____

_____

Text by Lois Rock
Illustrations copyright © 1997 Illustrator Louise Rawlings
This edition copyright © 1997 Lion Publishing
The author asserts the moral right
to be identified as the author of this work
Published by
Lion Publishing plc
Sandy Lane West, Oxford, England
ISBN 0 7459 3732 2
Lion Publishing
4050 Lee Vance View, Colorado Springs, CO 80918, USA
ISBN 0 7459 3732 2
First edition 1997
10 9 8 7 6 5 4 3 2 1 0

NIGHTLIGHTS

ALL YEAR LONG

LOIS ROCK

ILLUSTRATED BY LOUISE RAWLINGS

A LION BOOK

Where is the world in winter?
The leaves have left the trees,
And in the brown-grey garden
No flowers, no humming bees.

When the world is cold
I like to feel safe and warm.

When the world is dark
I like to feel safe and warm.

When the winter is long
I like to feel safe and warm.

The clouds, like giant pillows,
Toss feathers made of snow
To all the winds, who twirl them
Upon the world below.

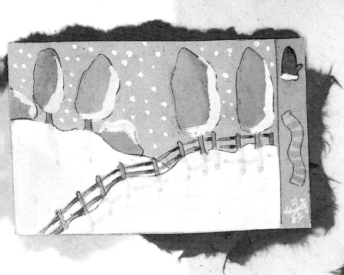

When snow falls
The world is so lovely.

When frost sparkles
The world is so lovely.

When the winter sky is
a bright, clear blue
The world is so lovely.

But then, a green shoot pushes
Up through the cold, hard ground
And reaches for the sunshine
That sparkles all around.

Something new is
happening:
The year is waking.

Something new is
happening:
The plants are
growing.

Something new is
happening:
The sun is warming
the world.

Next comes a leaf, a bud, a flower:
The world has turned to spring.
The blossom is like laughter
In trees where bright birds sing.

Springtime:
Listen to the birds.

Springtime:
Look at the flowers.

Springtime:
Animals are busy
with their babies.

The time has come to dig the earth,
To plant seeds, dark and small,
And leave them where worms wriggle
And silver raindrops fall.

Such tiny seeds.
Will they ever grow?

They need soft soil.
Will they ever grow?

They need gentle rain.
Will they ever grow?

The sun shines bright and
warms the earth:
The seeds begin to grow.
Behind the flowers on bush and tree,
Sweet fruits of summer show.

Look very close:
Seedlings with tiny,
green hands.

Look very close:
Tiny apples on the
apple tree.

Look very close:
Strawberries, ripe
and ready to eat.

Out in the rolling fields of corn,
The green blades turn to gold
The ripening ear bursts open—
There's more grain than it can hold.

The golden harvest:
It is so lovely to look at.

The golden harvest:
It is so lovely to eat.

The golden harvest:
It tells us the world
is good.

A harvest soon is gathered in
Of root and fruit and seed:
The precious crops that give us food
And everything we need.

For harvest
crops:
**We give
thanks.**

For food to
enjoy:
**We give
thanks.**

For good things
to share:
**We give
thanks.**

Quite soon the leaves turn red and gold,
But then they blow away
The colours of the seasons fade
To softly sleeping grey.

Why are there seasons?
That's the way the world was made.

Why are there seasons?
God made the world that way.

Why are there seasons?
God made the world to be our safe and lovely home.

Give thanks to God, who made the world,
The darkness and the light;
Who wakes the seasons, each in turn;

For the world:
We thank you, God.

For day and night:
We thank you, God.

For each lovely year:
We thank you, God.

who gives us sleep.
Goodnight.